**BUS**

# McKinsey & Company

**2005 Edition**

*Helping you make smarter career decisions.*

## WetFeet, Inc.

The Folger Building

101 Howard Street

Suite 300

San Francisco, CA 94105

Phone: (415) 284-7900 or 1-800-926-4JOB

Fax: (415) 284-7910

Website: www.WetFeet.com

## McKinsey & Company

ISBN: 1-58207-447-X

# Table of Contents

# McKinsey at a Glance

## Headquarters

55 East 52nd Street
21st Floor
New York, NY 10022
Phone: 212-446-7000
Fax: 212-446-8575
www.mckinsey.com

## Key Differentiating Factors

- Seen (and sees itself) as the world's most successful and influential management consulting firm

- Famous for its strong network and strong culture—there's definitely a McKinsey way to do things

- Focuses primarily on strategy and operations work

- Boasts of working primarily with clients' top management

## In the Recruiter's Words

"Getting a job at McKinsey isn't about crafting the perfect resume. Honors, promotions, test scores, and other academic achievements are meaningful, but they don't mean everything. We look for people who value excellence and are always working to achieve it."

"You must be exceptional in some way to move forward."

## In the Interview

- McKinsey is looking for people who are willing to challenge conventional wisdom. Don't kowtow to your interviewer, even when questions are aggressive.

- McKinsey weighs a candidate's leadership credentials heavily. Be prepared to describe in detail an experience where you took a leadership role, including all responsibilities you handled and any challenges you faced.

- Practice your case questions. McKinsey wants to see your problem-solving skills in action. Work out your case-question bugs in practice sessions before the interview.

## What Insiders Say

"I have a lot of autonomy in being able to define what I want my career to be and how to play it out. I also like McKinsey's commitment to personal and professional development."

"Clients don't bring us easy problems. There are no easy problems here. . . . There are no easy wins."

"There's so much flexibility in terms of what I could do with my time that the challenge is figuring out what the right path is. It's not a well defined 'do A, B, and C.' I have to decide what I want to do, convince people that what I'm doing makes sense, and find the resources to do it."

"Everyone believes that the people here are top quality. There's the assumption that everyone here is your equal. There aren't a lot of people here who are considered dead weight, which is exciting."

"It's an intense job, and it doesn't really let up. This level of intensity over an extended period can get difficult."

## The Career Ladder

- College graduates enter as business analysts.

- MBAs and other advanced-degree hires enter as associates.

## Personnel Highlights, 2004

Number of professionals, worldwide: more than 6,200

Number of professionals, U.S.: more than 1,700

## Estimated Global Hires, 2003–04

Undergrad hires: 275

MBA hires: 300

Summer MBA hires: 300

Experienced hires: 425

## Estimated U.S. Compensation, 2003–04

Starting salary, undergrads: $53,000, plus profit sharing and performance-based bonus at year-end

Starting salary, MBAs: $100,000 in first full year plus performance-based bonus

Note: Grad school financing is now offered only to associates asked to stay on.

**Source: WetFeet research.**

# The Firm

- Overview

- Industry Position

- A Quick History Lesson

- Organization of the Firm

- Recent Client List

- Typical Studies

- What's Hot

# Overview

When he took over McKinsey & Company after founder James O. McKinsey's death in 1937, Marvin Bower more or less invented the management consulting industry. And with his passing in 2003, he left behind what is now arguably the most powerful and intellectually formidable firm in the business.

The Firm (as it is affectionately called) may have taken a couple of hits in recent years, and highly respected competitors such as Bain and Booz Allen Hamilton may be nipping at its heels, but McKinsey remains, year after year, the most sought-after job in the world by MBAs. McKinsey's standards are sky high, the work is demanding, and the lifestyle is unrelenting. But the rewards, both financial and experiential, are hard to beat.

McKinsey's reputation is built on a long history of providing strategic advice to the top management of the world's largest corporations. The firm knows more CEOs on a first-name basis than perhaps any other organization. McKinsey alumni are influential movers and shakers in the business world, in the political sphere, and in nonprofit and development organizations. A stint at McKinsey can open many doors, including the one to the CEO suite. In fact, more than 70 past and present CEOs at Fortune 500 companies—Lou Gerstner of IBM, Philip Purcell of Morgan Stanley, Leo Mullin of Delta Air Lines, Kevin Sharer of Amgen, as well as the infamous ex-chief of Enron, Jeffrey Skilling—once worked for McKinsey.

Although McKinsey may well be the world's most prestigious management consulting firm, it is by no means the largest. The firm currently employs around 6,200 consultants worldwide and operates 82 offices (plus 27 business technology offices) in 44 countries. Whereas a decade or two ago the company might have felt intimate and clubby, it now feels much larger. And if you work in one of the bigger offices, don't expect to know everyone you pass in the halls on a first-name basis.

## Recent History

A great deal of expansion occurred during the late '90s tech bubble, and the firm has spent the last few years quietly trying to shed a few pounds by moving "out" (as opposed to up) a much greater proportion of its staff than it had historically. The numbers seem to have stabilized now, so competition to stay on the "up" track is now merely intense, as opposed to ruthless. Even McKinsey's new managing director, Ian Davis, admits a little overzealousness during the dot-com frenzy. As he told the *Financial Times* (perhaps understating the case), "On the dot-com Richter madness scale, we were probably a two out of 10. We weren't a 10 out of 10. Should any similar business frenzy occur again, we want to make sure it's nought, or one."

The firm has an unrivaled depth of experience. Given the sheer number of engagements it takes, there is a good chance that McKinsey has prior experience in any given situation. Critics charge that this can lead to a cookie-cutter approach to solving business problems, but even competitors acknowledge the formidable intellectual capital of the firm. Traditionally McKinsey has been able to bank on its big brains, charging a premium of up to 25 percent over its competitors. But as budgets get tighter, companies are inviting more consulting firms to face off in pitches. The unofficial word is that even McKinsey is offering deep discounts to land business it might have easily won unopposed in the past.

The firm's pristine image may have been tarnished a bit in recent years due in part to its intimate associations with notorious failures such as Enron and WorldCom, though the firm adamantly distances itself from these companies' more dubious dealings. And a period of overexpansion during the bubble years left the firm a bit bloated and in the rare position of having to aggressively cut costs. The storied spare-no-expense retreats and lavish lifestyle have been tempered, and some perks have been reeled in. Yet those who can cut the mustard and survive McKinsey's unblinking up-or-out dictum will still find themselves handsomely rewarded.

While McKinsey's place at the top of the consulting heap appears secure, the heap itself may be shrinking. The industry contracted about 2 percent in 2003 and 6 percent the year before. Companies that once thought nothing of throwing untold millions of dollars into strategy documents—documents that were often contested internally or that went partially or wholly unimplemented—are thinking twice about such decadent expenditures. Instead, consultants are being engaged for shorter projects that are more focused on specific problems, often more operational than strategic. "We went through a company's invoices one by one looking for ways to cut costs," says one insider. And the firm's fees may not be quite as eye popping as they once were. In addition, some companies are developing the capabilities in-house, even raiding the top consulting firms for talent. McKinsey and its competitors are feeling the effects of these industry-wide trends.

## Working @McKinsey?

Whatever the current trends and troubles, McKinsey is still the premier opportunity in the industry. As one insider put it, "When I look around at my friends in other places, I still think this is by far the best place to be." McKinsey is fiercely committed to the people it hires and to their development. In 2002, when analysts greatly outnumbered engagements, McKinsey honored its 2-year commitment to its business analysts in New York. Taking advantage of the downtime, McKinsey provided numerous resume-writing workshops and made its extraordinary network and research resources available to all outgoing staffers. And having that McKinsey name on the resume is still a surefire door opener.

While McKinsey still draws more staff from the top business schools than from any other background, MBAs actually account for fewer than half of all hires these days. The firm's professional staff includes a growing number of PhDs, MDs, and JDs, and the firm has begun to recruit more specialists to augment its strong staff of generalists.

In the new fiscal reality, McKinsey's legendary parties and perks have been scaled back. Luxury ski weekends may be replaced by nice dinners. Some insiders feel that fewer social events decrease camaraderie with your analyst class, but there's plenty of time to bond as you burn the midnight oil together on a demanding project. In the past, McKinsey reimbursed all analyst alumni for their business-school expenses; these days only those who are asked to return to the firm can expect such largesse. Insiders have also reported cutbacks on support services—meaning you may have to put together your own PowerPoint presentations. You will, however, still get a free cell phone (the better for your superiors and coworkers to reach you on a Saturday night).

If you're looking to land a job at McKinsey, expect stiff competition, particularly at the business analyst level where standards are extremely high. Just about everyone who wants to be a consultant—and some people who don't—wind up interviewing with McKinsey. And if you do survive the interview process, you will constantly be challenged to improve your performance and develop new skills. The firm's hard-nosed up-or-out policy leaves little room for laggards. But the firm does its part to assist in your career growth. In the New York office, for example, a professional development coordinator provides career

> **At any McKinsey office in the world, the culture is very similar. A McKinsey person is a McKinsey person, no matter where they are.**

guidance and assistance in pursuing a track that is most rewarding to you. "There's almost too much hand-holding," says one insider. Expect regular feedback and the opportunity to learn from pros. "People feel comfortable asking all the time, 'How am I doing?'" says an insider. Says another: "McKinsey at its core is an apprenticeship model. You learn from the people around you; you learn from the partners."

Despite McKinsey's many appealing attributes, the firm is not for everyone. The exclusive (some say arrogant) culture that it cultivates is sure to rub some people the wrong way. Some say McKinsey's "one firm" way of doing things can stifle individuality—not to mention take up a good bit of your personal life. One insider says, "At any McKinsey office in the world, the culture is very similar. A McKinsey person is a McKinsey person, no matter where they are." Another insider says, "The people are amazing, but sometimes I wish it was a little more hip. It's pretty square." And as the organization has grown bigger, insiders acknowledge that it is not as intimate as it once was. The upside of the firm's size: If you are interested in a particular industry or a functional focus (strategy, operations, systems), there's an excellent chance that McKinsey will house some of the leading authorities in the field. Given the size and structure of the firm, you might not meet these experts personally, but McKinsey nonetheless encourages employees to reach out to them for advice and support. And that's a resource unique to McKinsey.

3 1833 04819 2873

## Competitive Strategy

McKinsey's competitive strategy is surprisingly simple. According to a quotation in Tom Peters' book *Crazy Times Call for Crazy Organizations*, it boils down to this: "We're smarter than everyone else, and that's enough to maintain our advantage." (Few would call McKinsey humble.) But the firm is smart enough to know that it can't be complacent. McKinsey is constantly trying to widen the scope of its services and enter new segments of the consulting market. Relatively new disciplines include mergers and acquisitions, information technology, and brand consulting. (Predictably, the firm's initiatives in the e-commerce/e-transformation business have cooled considerably.) This broader range of services goes along neatly with the firm's traditional strategy practice.

## The Bottom Line

McKinsey is the 800-pound gorilla on the consulting block. Whether you're gunning for the partner track or just planning to spend 2 or 3 years with the firm before heading off to greener pastures (well, maybe not greener, but certainly more livable), McKinsey offers some of the best experience, opportunity, and professional development in the industry—not to mention being a big plus on any resume.

But you don't get all of that for nothing. Work and travel are extremely demanding, hours are long, and McKinsey is more structured than some of its smaller competitors. To survive, you'll be required to put the firm and its work before your personal life. In return, the company will treat you exceedingly well— especially if you like big salaries, expensive offices, and first-class accommodations. If you like the perks and don't mind doing everything the McKinsey way, it's a great place to work for undergrads, MBAs, and an assortment of other advanced-degree holders.

# Industry Position

Perhaps the largest and most renowned pure management consulting firm in the world, McKinsey faces relentless competition from a whole pack of hungry firms (Bain, Booz Allen, BCG, Mercer, et al.) that hire the same type of people and do similar high-quality work. When all is said and done, however, McKinsey's reputation precedes it: Among strategy firms, McKinsey ranked first in revenue for 2003, according to *Consultants News*. Within the overall management consulting field, *Consultants News* ranks McKinsey eighth in revenue, down a notch from last year. It trails a number of big systems integration houses, some of which are subsidiaries of technology manufacturers.

## Other Rankings

In *Consulting Magazine's* 2003 ranking of the best consulting firms to work for, McKinsey showed up in second place for the third year running, this year behind Bain & Company. One respondent calls McKinsey "an environment unparalleled in business, where one can create opportunities to learn, to grow, and to advance based on their passions and their performance." The report delivers familiar tales of long days and endless travel and asserts that the firm remains committed to investing in the development of its employees. It has been pointed out that working in almost any consulting firm is, compared to most other jobs, a rather masochistic way to make a living. But for you masochists, clearly you could do a lot worse than McKinsey.

|  20 Largest Consulting Firms, by 2003 Consulting Revenue | |
| --- | --- |
| **Rank** | **Firm** |
| 1 | IBM |
| 2 | Accenture |
| 3 | Deloitte |
| 4 | Capgemini |
| 5 | CSC |
| 6 | BearingPoint |
| 7 | Hewlett-Packard |
| **8** | **McKinsey & Co.** |
| 9 | Mercer |
| 10 | SAP |
| 11 | T-Systems |
| 12 | Booz Allen Hamilton |
| 13 | LogicaCMG |
| 14 | Atos Origin |
| 15 | Oracle |
| 16 | Unisys |
| 17 | Altran |
| 18 | EDS |
| 19 | TietoEnator |
| 20 | Watson Wyatt Worldwide |

Source: Excerpted and reprinted with permission of *Consultants News* June 2004; *Consultants News*/Kennedy Information, Peterborough, NH 03458 USA; phone: 800-531-0007; www.ConsultingCentral.com.

## The Student Perspective

Industry publications may change their rankings from year to year, but students have been consistent in their opinion of McKinsey. For 8 years running, MBAs surveyed by Universum have ranked McKinsey the number-one place they'd like to work. Boston Consulting Group, Bain & Company, and Coca Cola were next on the list.

| Consulting Firms that Ranked in the Top 50 | |
| --- | --- |
| **Rank** | **Firm** |
| 1 | McKinsey & Co. |
| 4 | IBM |
| 7 | Bain & Co. |
| 10 | Booz Allen Hamilton |
| 11 | Deloitte |
| 13 | Boston Consulting Group |
| 27 | Accenture |

Source: Based on a study by Universum, published in *Fortune*. Ann Harrington, *Fortune*, 4/19/2004.

# A Quick History Lesson

While the firm's namesake is James O. McKinsey, who first opened shop in 1926, its true founder is Marvin Bower, a Harvard MBA and JD hired by McKinsey. Bower opened a new office shortly after McKinsey's death to run Marshall Field & Co. Despite being the firm's leader in every sense, Bower retained the McKinsey name because he didn't want the bother and distraction that comes from having one's own name on the door. And with that, Bower set about creating an industry. He valued intellectual integrity above all else, and he laid down a set of guiding principles on which the firm would run. He wanted to create an organization that maintained the professionalism (and fee structure) of a law firm, but provided its clients—preferably top executives—with advice about managing their businesses. Bower actively managed the firm for more than 30 years, defining much of what we know today as McKinsey culture (e.g., commitment to the client and insistence that men wear long socks), and guided the firm in new business directions.

Since Bower's departure in the late '60s, McKinsey has been led by a succession of managing directors, elected to 3-year terms by senior directors. These leaders have helped the firm increase its annual revenue from $20 million to more than $3 billion. They've also witnessed the growth of hungry competitors, including Bain, BCG, and Booz Allen; double-digit annual compound growth in the industry through much of the '90s; the rise and fall of the dot com; and the transforming effects of technology on the industry. Ian Davis became McKinsey's newest managing director in July 2003, replacing Rajat Gupta.

Marvin Bower passed away in 2003 at the age of 99.

# Organization of the Firm

## View from the Top

McKinsey may still be organized as a partnership, but this is no backyard Ben & Jerry's organization where everybody knows the head partners and their families. In 1994, McKinsey's partner ranks had swelled so much that the firm had to file for an exemption with the Securities and Exchange Commission, which usually limits partnerships to 500. Even with the firm's continued growth, McKinsey is a far smaller organization than most of its clients. Still, don't expect to have a one-on-one with the managing director during your first week in the office.

McKinsey's executive pyramid still looks more like a partnership than a traditional, hierarchical Fortune 500 firm. Favoring a nonhierarchical corporate structure, McKinsey has long rejected the traditional CEO/chairman-type designation for its leaders. Instead, a managing director—elected for a 3-year term by a group of 150 or so senior partners—heads up the firm. The present managing director, Ian Davis, a Brit, assumed his post in 2003, replacing Rajat Gupta.

## View from the Middle

McKinsey touts its "one firm" approach, which holds that individual offices come second to the firm as a whole and are generally de-emphasized when dealing with profits or making decisions. A few insiders who have transferred offices tell us that things are remarkably similar from one location to another, which allows for easy and frequent mobility between sites. In reality, there's a much better chance of seeing the partners (and maybe even having lunch with them) at the Charlotte office than there is in New York. McKinsey tries to combat the perception that it's a huge, impersonal organization by pointing out that most of its offices employ fewer than 100 people.

## View from the Bottom

McKinsey believes it can produce greater value for clients if consultants work on one engagement (McKinsey-speak for project) at a time. As at other firms, engagements are handled by teams. The composition of project teams at McKinsey depends in part on the scope and focus of the engagement. Many engagements are staffed with people from several different McKinsey offices. A typical engagement can last between 2 and 6 months and commonly involves three to six consultants. While some engagements may last for over a year, the trend is toward shorter engagements. McKinsey typically uses fewer client members on its teams than many other consulting firms, especially competitors who focus on implementation work, such as Accenture. One other difference is that McKinsey prides itself on working with clients' top management. If you prefer to roll up your sleeves and interact with the working stiffs at the client site, you might be better off at one of the Big Five firms.

## McKinsey's Industry and Functional Practices

The following is a list of the firm's industry and functional practices as of summer 2004. These practices change periodically to better fit customer needs. Practices generally comprise specific service offerings. For instance, the business building practice offers the following services: growth and innovation, new business start-up, technology management, innovative communities, and new ventures. Insurance services includes asset management, reinsurance, IT insurance, and mRisk: Insurance e-Commerce. For additional information, see www.mckinsey.com/clientservice.

## Industry Practices

Automotive and assembly

Banking and securities

Chemicals

Consumer packaged goods

Electric power and natural gas

High-tech

Insurance

Media and entertainment

Metals and mining

Nonprofit

Payor/provider

Petroleum

Pharmaceuticals and medical products

Private equity

Pulp and paper/forest products

Retail

Telecommunications

Travel and logistics

## Functional Practices

Business technology office

Corporate finance

Marketing and sales

Operations

Organization

Strategy

# Recent Client List

Consulting firms hate to part with the names of their clients, but we managed to get a few anyway. Here are a few companies McKinsey has worked with:

Aeroflot

Amdahl Corp.

American Express

AOL Time Warner

Armco

AT&T

Arrow Electronics

Bank of England

BBC

CBS

Daimler-Benz

Delta Airlines

Enron

Frito-Lay

FMC

General Electric

General Motors

Global Crossing Ltd.

Government of Mexico

Government of Switzerland

Government of Taiwan

Hewlett-Packard

Home Depot

IBM

Intermountain Health Care

International Telecommunications Union

Johnson & Johnson

K Mart

Kaiser Permanente

KLM Royal Dutch Airlines

Kodak

Lever Brothers

Los Angeles Public Schools

Mellon Bank

Mitsubishi Corp.

NBC News

New York Public Schools

New York State Council on the Arts

Oxford University

Pacific Telesis

PepsiCo

RJR Nabisco

Royal Dutch Shell

Sears Roebuck & Co.

Siemens

State Industrial and Investment Corp. of Maharashtra

SwissAir Group

The Vatican

# Typical Studies

## Magazine Study

The firm devised a strategy to increase advertising revenues for a leading consumer magazine title. It analyzed the target audience and looked for the most relevant advertising segments for that audience. The plan would increase revenue by 5 percent, at a time when most other titles are seeing a roughly 10 percent decline in advertising dollars.

## Book Publishing Study

At a major publisher, McKinsey reviewed the book-publishing process, from start to finish. It looked at manuscript screening, editing, typesetting, printing, and so on, and identified ways to streamline the process. McKinsey was able to halve the time it takes to bring a book to market.

## Emergency Response Study

In the wake of 9/11, McKinsey conducted an analysis for the New York City Chamber of Commerce to determine the impact the event would have on the city. It made a number of recommendations to the city and state about necessary responses to the tragedy. While this study may not be typical, turning to McKinsey for analysis when the stakes are high is.

## Medical Device Study

The firm completed a study for a medical device company that faced a change in its core markets as a result of changing medical technology. The study identified the best future opportunities in the U.S. and global markets and offered recommendations for strategic alliances.

## Bank Operations Study

McKinsey analyzed the backroom costs of a major retail bank to find out why it was experiencing ongoing cost increases. It discovered that the problem was an outdated process and recommended a new organizational design that would enable the bank to identify processing bottlenecks, shorten cycle times, lower costs, and reduce inventory. McKinsey worked with the bank to create an implementation team. The engagement resulted in productivity improvements and decreased customer wait times.

## Recruiting Study

McKinsey worked with a Scandinavian natural resources conglomerate to conduct an organizational talent review, which the firm positioned as a "leadership development process." The program involved a review process, data evaluation, and the presentation of findings to top executives, and it resulted in the company's first open reorganization of several top positions.

## Chicago Technology Study

McKinsey worked with the city of Chicago on a technology initiative. The firm drew on Chicago's assets, including strong public transportation and numerous educational institutions, to make recommendations for growing Chicago's technology businesses.

# What's Hot

## The Nonprofit Practice

McKinsey started a nonprofit practice in 2000, building on its 75-year history of service to local nonprofits around the world. McKinsey believes that working with nonprofits expands the opportunities for its consultants to give back to their communities and is important to their professional development. Each year, the firm's nonprofit work represents an in-kind contribution of well over $100 million, serving more than 200 nonprofit and public-sector clients in a range of areas including social service, environment, economic development, international aid and development, and arts and culture organizations. The firm has also dedicated leadership to building new knowledge specific to the nonprofit sector and identifying and disseminating nonprofit managerial best practices. Insiders are very excited about this work, and McKinsey claims that over half of its consultants will work with nonprofits at some point in their careers. "At a local office level, we continue to be devoted to high-impact nonprofit and pro bono work." For instance, in the wake of 9/11, the New York office worked on nine separate pro bono assignments including serving the Lower Manhattan Development Corporation, overseeing the development of a victim database for New York State Attorney General Elliot Spitzer, and studying how New York Police Department and Fire Department members reacted during the World Trade Center attacks. McKinsey was also involved in an effort to bring medical treatment to a greater portion of Uganda's AIDS-ravaged population. Check out McKinsey's website to find out more about some of these projects.

## Business Technology Office

Founded in 1997, the BTO provides strategy consulting with a distinctive technological bent to senior management teams. McKinsey is quick to point out that the BTO is not an integration house and does not do applications development. Rather, it develops strategies for using technology to make better investments and gain market share. The BTO works as a global office, operating in 27 cities in 19 countries: Silicon Valley, East Coast (Stamford, New York), Chicago, Montreal, Toronto, London, Zurich, Cologne, Dusseldorf, Frankfurt, Gothenburg, Hamburg, Stuttgart, Vienna, Amsterdam, Copenhagen, Helsinki, Oslo, Stockholm, Madrid, Lisbon, Milan, Paris, Eastern Europe (Budapest, Warsaw, Prague), Mercosur (Buenos Aires, Sao Paulo), and Southeast Asia (Singapore, Seoul, Hong Kong).

McKinsey expects to have more than 500 BTO consultants by next year, and recruiting continues to grow apace with client demands. Those looking to land a job at a BTO office need the traditional top-notch McKinsey credentials (an MBA or other advanced degree, plus hands-on experience with a tech company or an IT consulting firm). About 50 percent of BTO hires come from industry, while the rest are recruited on campus. The BTO is a particularly good choice for those who have been doing technical implementation but would like more strategy work.

# On the Job

- Business Analysts
- Associates

# Business Analysts

On the Job

McKinsey recruits and hires a large crop of business analysts from leading undergraduate programs around the world. In fact, because of its size, McKinsey typically hires more undergrads than any other elite consulting firm. As an analyst you can expect to be thrown into the workflow from day one, so bring your life-jacket. "As an analyst, the more willing you are to work independently, the more success you'll have," says an insider. Says another, "McKinsey places a lot of value on the analyst experience, treating analysts as colleagues rather than as grunt resources." One analyst was amazed by the kind of exposure the job pro-vided. "I was quoted in the *New York Times*, the *New York Post*, and the *Washington Post*." Another says, "I was a bit surprised at the level of work. We work a lot. Compared to I-banks, it's a better lifestyle. Nights aren't 2 a.m., they're midnight. But coming from an academic background, it's a shift. Be ready for that."

As a key member of the McKinsey crew, you will

- Conduct field research.
- Meet with customers and conduct interviews.
- Analyze operations (develop process-flow diagrams, spreadsheet analysis, etc.).
- Work with clients to produce necessary data for studies.
- Present research to team.
- Build economic models (spreadsheets).
- Conduct market segmentation studies (identify key markets for products or services and determine their size).

## A Day in the Life of an Analyst

9:00   Arrive at office, the *New York Times* in hand.

9:05   Finish latté and bagel while reading newspaper.

9:15   Team meeting to discuss current status of telecom company project. Discuss progress others have made and determine what I need to do next. It's important to understand who is doing what, so that all efforts are in synch. It's also important to find out what others are learning.

10:15  Present results of latest profit data dump and analysis from accounting department. This is part of the project I'm responsible for. I talked to the accounting department to learn the profit margins and analyzed that information.

11:15  Prescheduled call from telecom manager to discuss last month's sales. What will people pay for the products? Now that I know the profits, I can begin to find out what adjustments in price would mean. If we cut prices a little and sales soar, economies of scale could make this firm a windfall. That's what my gut is saying. Of course, if we raise prices without a drop in sales that would be a win, too.

12:00  Check in with librarian to track down last industry study. I read it as I wander over to the lunchroom and find some information that supports my gut.

12:15  Lunch with team in conference room. We talk about the project. A lot of information gets passed back and forth in informal settings; lunch is a good place to try out ideas.

12:45  Prepare first draft of 30 sales and pricing slides based on morning meeting. I want to lower the price a bit because the data suggests this will raise sales a bundle.

3:00   Meet with graphics person to arrange slide presentation. I want it to look really, really good.

> " "
>
> **McKinsey places a lot of value on the analyst experience, treating analysts as colleagues rather than as grunt resources.**

3:30   Arrange, with telecom production manager, three plant tours for next week. I want to get a better idea of how the equipment is manufactured.

4:00   Update work plan and circulate it to team members. In this business, you depend on others, so you need to keep everyone looped in.

5:00   Call Japan to arrange delivery of international customer questionnaires.

6:00   Continue working on slides.

8:00   Order in sushi.

8:45   Write up notes from day's findings.

9:30   Call up limo service for ride home.

# Associates

Advanced-degree hires, including MBAs, JDs, and PhDs, are called associates. Most of their time is spent working as an integral part of a project team. Insiders tell us that associates have responsibility for the following tasks:

- Leading brainstorming sessions with clients
- Preparing and giving presentations to team and to clients
- Conducting external research through library work, interviews, client-site work, and so on
- Laying out project work plan and assign tasks for team
- Training members of client team in analytical techniques or new approaches
- Synthesizing research into meaningful recommendations

## A Day in the Life of an Associate (JD)

8:00   Go straight to client's office—a prestigious New York bank. Give presentation on operational efficiency. We've been working directly with the CEO for the past couple months. I sit next to two top executives and tell them what I think; I answer their questions. It's astounding. Sometimes I feel like I don't even belong here.

12:30   Lunch with my team at Gramercy Park, one of New York's best restaurants. We talk about team dynamics and our workload and try to figure out why the workload is so heavy lately. Reassuringly, the director makes it clear that he finds our working past 10 p.m. unacceptable.

2:30   Return to office and check voice mail—13 messages. Four are from my fiancée, two are from a partner asking about a potential client, five are from friends, one is from a team assistant telling me that some documents that I faxed to her are ready, and one is from my engagement manager.

3:00    Check e-mail. I get between 20 and 40 e-mails a day. A lot of it is just because I'm part of the accelerator—I participate in a listserv that circulates questions. The knowledge exchange here is unparalleled—someone will ask a question I could never dream of having an answer to, and within 5 minutes someone comes up with an answer.

3:45    I read news websites: *Red Herring, Forbes, Bloomberg, CNN*, the *New York Times*. I'm sort of a news junkie.

4:30    Put together an agenda for a prioritization workshop I'm having with a client. We've identified various growth opportunities—new products and services and extensions of old ones—and we have to determine which to pursue.

5:30    Meet with my engagement manager to review the document and make edits.

7:00    Pack up my laptop and recharge the cell phone and PDA that the firm provides. I have a vacation day scheduled tomorrow, so I call it an early night and head home.

# The Workplace

- Lifestyle

- Culture

- Workplace Diversity

- Civic Involvement

- Compensation, Vacation, and Perks

- Career Path

- Training

- Insider Scoop

# Lifestyle

At McKinsey you'll be compensated very nicely for your work, you'll earn loads of frequent-flyer points, and you'll travel in style. But you'll also work a lot, travel a lot, and cancel your personal plans a lot. If you value your free time, think long and hard about whether the McKinsey lifestyle—and consulting in general—is right for you. Imagine an end-of-semester crunch when you have a project due for every class and finals start in 3 days. One insider says, "The lifestyle is always a challenge. It's always client first, and it's a bummer to check your voice mail at 9 p.m. and realize there's something you have to do before the morning. If you let it, work can consume you."

On top of that, everybody on your team (including you) is one of those over-achieving types who can't stand the thought of finishing second to anyone—ever. That said, insiders do report that some people within the firm are more responsive to lifestyle concerns than others. "It depends on your team," says one insider. "Some people expect more and believe in getting the work done no matter what it takes. Others are more lifestyle conscious." But even if you get assigned to a team that respects the fact that you exist outside of McKinsey, you can be sure that your personal life will suffer. As one insider says, "I had a friend who left mainly because he wanted to get married."

## Hours

McKinsey consultants at all levels report that hours vary greatly from day to day and week to week, depending on the project, the stage of the project, and the client. Serious crunch times can require lots of caffeine and 80-hour weeks; slow times may require only 40 to 45 hours a week. Between projects—when you're "on the beach," as consultants like to say—your time is pretty much your own, but don't count on getting out to the shore very often. On average, McKinsey consultants report working about 60 hours per week.

## Travel

McKinsey's recruiting brochures estimate that most consultants are on the road two nights per week, but the amount of travel required depends on the industry, the client, and the particular study. For example, consultants based in the New York headquarters working on a financial-services project may sleep at home (or at least locally) every night of the week. On the other hand, a colleague working with an out-of-town technology company will be raking in the frequent-flyer miles with her trips to the client site every Sunday night or Monday morning and return flights home late Thursday evenings—for weeks or months on end. (As a rule, McKinsey tries to have everyone back at the office on Fridays.) "I knew there was a lot of travel, but there was a *lot* of travel," says an insider about the way expectations compared to the actual new-hire experience. If you've always wanted a frequent-flyer gold card, you won't be disappointed. As one insider says, "Forget gold. Everyone here has platinum."

**" "**

**The lifestyle is always a challenge. It's always client first, and it's a bummer to check your voice mail at 9 p.m. and realize there's something you have to do before the morning. If you let it, work can consume you.**

# Culture

McKinsey's many foreign-born employees and its offices around the world give the firm a distinct international flavor. Insiders say there are differences from office to office, depending on location as much as the size of the office. That said, McKinsey strives to uphold a "one firm" image, so that every office and consultant will look and behave consistently, regardless of location. One insider says that Japanese documents from the Tokyo office look exactly like documents from the New York office and the Singapore office. McKinsey prides itself on its polished and professional image and requires that employees uphold that image through their actions, their bearing, and their dress. (You won't fit in if you're into dangly earrings, "expressive" haircuts, or nifty thrift-store finds.) Insiders admit that the place would never be described as hip.

Just as there may be differences from office to office, each project team may develop a vibe of its own. While some team leaders may be all business, others may encourage fun team-bonding activities. One insider described an enjoyable evening of team bonding that included a private room at a swanky restaurant and a bottle of expensive vodka.

Many insiders comment on the overall friendliness and supportiveness of their colleagues at McKinsey. One says, "I thought it would be very competitive. You always hear about 'up or out.' When I joined, I found that the people are definitely driven and ambitious, but they're friendly, and that was surprising." They are also quick to praise the intellectual talents of the firm's employees. "Everyone believes the people here are top quality. There's the assumption that everyone here is your equal. There aren't a lot of people who could be considered dead weight, which is exciting." Insiders also tend to share a belief that McKinsey hires a special group of people. McKinseyites believe that they are the best and brightest, and this supreme confidence is often interpreted by outside observers as arrogance.

The firm had been growing at a relatively rapid pace, but this trend seems to have reversed a bit recently. Still, the firm feels big. "McKinsey is struggling with its size," says one insider. "Many people remember when their office was small enough [that] you knew everyone. Now people don't recognize or know a lot of the people they pass in the hallways."

To compensate, McKinsey has been organizing more events within particular interest groups. For example, instead of taking the whole office on a retreat, many offices now organize events around classes of BAs or first-year associates. However, in terms of frequency and lavishness, these events pale in comparison to those of a couple years ago. An insider tells us that a task force has been created to reaffirm the firm's values. In training, McKinsey's culture is reinforced through stories, generally focused on client services, about the firm's past. Insiders say that larger offices, such as the New York office, have made a concerted effort to combat the negatives related to their size by hosting team-building events.

Dress at McKinsey is business casual. The office atmosphere could be termed "business subdued": polite, contained, efficient, and perhaps a little unnatural. "There aren't a lot of people scurrying," says an insider. "People in general are likely to stop and talk as they pass each other. It's not a very loud place compared to other offices I've been in. You don't hear a lot of people talking or loud conference calls with the doors open. Overall it's a fairly conservative work environment in terms of the way people act or dress. It's not that acting or dressing differently is frowned upon—it's that the way the culture has evolved is conservative. Not stuffy, I'd say."

A 2001 WetFeet survey of McKinsey interviewees was generally positive, although words such as "arrogance" were mentioned. There's clear respect both for the company and for the doors a job at McKinsey can open. One interviewee commented on how prompt and helpful the firm was in providing feedback as the interview process unfolded. Another liked the firm's candor, "I always felt like I was getting a straight answer." The firm also seems to have the recruiting process down: "At McKinsey, everything is tight. The recruiting process is very professional and organized." Of course, the firm will always have critics, deserved or not, as long as it's on top. Warned one interviewee, "I think most people go there because it's McKinsey, and not because it's necessarily the best place for them to go."

# Workplace Diversity

Some McKinsey employees complain that the firm is still largely white, male, and conservative—but it seems to be trying to change. "People are the major resource of this firm, and we can't afford to lose people disproportionately [in terms of race and gender]. This has been a difficult problem for years . . . but we're working on it," says an insider. McKinsey does have hiring programs to recruit women and minority candidates, as well as a formal mechanism for investigating and addressing workplace issues related to harassment and discrimination. The firm hosts on-campus gay and lesbian recruiting dinners—a rarity in the industry. Also, the firm extends domestic-partner health benefits to both same-sex and opposite-sex domestic partners.

McKinsey has formal ties to organizations such as the National Black MBA Association, A Better Chance, Catalyst, and the National Society of Black Engineers. The firm sponsors an annual networking conference for minority consultants to help them focus on professional and skill development. An insider says, "Diversity is definitely important to McKinsey. They think carefully about it and they're trying to raise the bar in those areas."

## Opportunities for Women

McKinsey hires a large number of women at junior levels, but, as is common in the industry, not many make it to the top. "I think the firm still has a way to go," says an insider. Says another, "The lifestyle is not conducive to work/family balance, and we have a problem retaining women at the senior level. McKinsey has tried to be compromising and innovative about part-time work and extended leaves, but keeping women around as partners or directors is a challenge." As of

> **I've never really gotten the sense that McKinsey is a sexist place. Sometimes our clients are sexist, but people within the firm do a good job of making sure the clients treat everyone with respect.**

2000, just 15 percent of U.S. principals were female. Efforts toward retaining women include family-friendly policies such as 10-week full-pay maternity leave in the United States (local laws govern the policy in other countries), longer unpaid leaves of absence for parents, adoption assistance, and part-time work options (nearly three-quarters of the firm's part-time consultants are women). An insider says that the New York office has a special room set aside for breastfeeding mothers. The firm also sponsors both formal and informal women's gatherings—every 2 years it holds a worldwide women's conference that gathers female McKinsey consultants to discuss pertinent issues. And the firm has developed programs—such as Men and Women as Professional Colleagues—intended to foster a working environment that is friendly to both genders.

One female insider says, "I've never really gotten the sense that McKinsey is a sexist place. Sometimes our clients are sexist, but people within the firm do a good job of making sure the clients treat everyone with respect. I've never felt there were things I couldn't or shouldn't do because I'm a woman."

# Civic Involvement

McKinsey encourages employee participation in civic activities. "In fact," says one insider, "on performance reviews, one of the things they consider is how active you were in community service." Periodically, consultants will have the opportunity to work full-time with a case team on pro bono projects for non-profit organizations; in fact, the firm devotes about 5 percent of its labor hours to pro bono work. Occasionally, an office may close for the day to perform community service. In addition, most offices sponsor nonprofit groups and charitable organizations chosen by the office staff. The New York office, for example, has sponsored the Boys Choir of Harlem, a community service day, and New York Cares, an organization that coordinates volunteer opportunities throughout the city.

# Compensation, Vacation, and Perks

McKinsey pays its people well. The firm hadn't determined its salary scale for 2003–04 at press time, but sources indicate that compensation will remain stable in relation to last year. The average first-year compensation for MBAs hired from U.S. campuses in 2002–03 was $160,000. Undergraduates hired from U.S. campuses started at $55,000 to $60,000. It is unclear whether signing bonuses will be offered this year, but you can be sure McKinsey's offers will be competitive with other top firms.

Undergraduates are eligible for frequent raises; base salary can increase by 10 to 20 percent every 6 months. One insider says, "The analyst role is more of a learning experience, and they want to reward you if you demonstrate that you've learned a lot in the last months." Insiders note that by their second year most undergraduates will be making between $66,000 and $78,000 a year. Both undergraduates and MBAs receive profit sharing and full benefits as part of their compensation packages. While all undergraduates historically received automatic graduate school financing, this year it is only being offered to those analysts who are asked to stay on (see "Career Path").

U.S. employees start with 3 weeks of vacation and receive an additional week after 2 years of service. (Benefits vary from country to country.) The unwritten rule is that employees have a good deal of flexibility between projects.

McKinsey is definitely the king of the do-right-by-your-employees school of thought. In a good year, that includes chichi weekends and blow-out shindigs for consultants and their significant others at famous resorts and vacation spots around the world. At the local level, the firm provides free drinks and food for employees. You also get a cell phone, and if you don't go above the allotted minutes you don't need to itemize your calls. McKinsey also provides a very generous relocation allowance for new employees and their families, as well as a number of generous savings and pension plans, and has an unwritten policy of giving departing employees a bonus package and job search support. When more consultants than usual were asked to move on last year, sources reported that the firm was extremely generous with job search assistance, holding resume-writing workshops and hiring an outplacement firm.

# Career Path

There seem to be two approaches to working for McKinsey. The first approach is to sign on, hunker down, and work your butt off to make it to partner. Given the competition, you have to work exceptionally hard, dabble in the political game, and count on getting a few great breaks in the process, such as high-profile assignments. The second approach (taken by some who were initially shooting for the partner track) is to sign on, work hard for a few years, learn a lot, add the McKinsey name to your resume, and then move on to another firm or a startup. Dilbert may joke about consultants' ability to run an organization, but insiders tell us that those who have worked at McKinsey are hot properties in the job market. And McKinsey itself is quick to point out the strength and value of its alumni network, now over 8,000 strong.

An insider says about the firm's up-or-out policy, "We expect people to grow and take on more as they stay with McKinsey. We won't allow people to be associates for 3 or 4 years. We view it as inconsistent with our values and our goals of developing people. You have to move up, or we don't encourage you to stay." However, the up-or-out policy was recently modified. A new personal readiness policy allows people to move up sooner or later than dictated by the traditional advancement time frame. But, keep in mind, that insiders report there is not a lot of room for slow advancers in the more austere current climate. And talent is just one of many indicators of success in the firm. "How much you enjoy the work and how much time you want to spend doing it are definitely factors that determine whether you stay on," says an insider. In other words, if you're just going through the motions, no matter how successfully, you're better off getting out—and probably will be "counseled out" anyway.

McKinsey starts consultants out as generalists, but as you progress at McKinsey you'll begin to specialize by function and industry. Insiders tell us that pressure to specialize sooner is mounting, due to fewer projects and more intense competition. As you proceed through your career you will have a say in which projects you get. VOX, the firm's preference-based staffing system, provides a view of all engagements throughout the world. You won't be guaranteed an assignment, but the system records your preferences, and as your skills grow so will your influence over what you do. Here too, current realities have limited consultants' ability to pick and choose as freely as they might once have.

The firm makes a big effort to ensure that all consultants are mentored. Twice a year a professional development coordinator meets with each consultant for an evaluation and is the go-to for questions about development issues. Also, as an insider says, "You're encouraged to find as many informal mentors as you can." Apparently the firm conducts a survey every 6 months. Consultants record the names of their mentors; the resulting list is circulated among partners, and it's embarrassing for those who aren't named. "As soon as you begin to get comfortable, McKinsey gives you more things that make you uncomfortable," says an insider. But you get a lot of support: "There are really a lot of people here who care a lot about being good mentors."

## Opportunities for Undergraduates

Undergraduates are typically hired as business analysts. Although there is flexibility in the length of this program, business analysts usually stay for about 2 years. At the end of 2 years, some analysts will stay for an additional year, perhaps signing up for an overseas stint. A select number of the most talented analysts in a class will be offered the opportunity to stay at the firm and become associates, achieving a rank equivalent to business school hires. The bulk of analysts, however, will leave after 2 years to enroll in a graduate school program or take a job at another firm. McKinsey will sponsor all analysts who wish to attend business-related graduate school (which includes law school as well as B-school). If you return to McKinsey as an associate after completing a program, your debt to the company will be forgiven over a 2-year period. If you choose to leave the firm before your 2 years are up, the amount of sponsorship you received will be treated as a loan that must be repaid (prorated according to the amount of time worked at McKinsey after grad school).

## Opportunities for MBAs

Most new MBA hires start as associates. Those on the "up" track usually begin managing teams within 2 to 3 years, but the firm's new personal readiness policy means that promotion may happen sooner. Advancement to principal usually takes place 5 to 7 years after joining the firm, and promotion to director may occur after an additional 5 to 6 years. Although there are examples of rapid ascension up the corporate ladder (e.g., former managing director Rajat Gupta), such cases are much less common at McKinsey than at smaller, faster-growing firms such as Mercer or Bain. People who don't make the grade (i.e., those on the "out" track), or who tire of the consulting life, are encouraged to leave for other pastures. McKinsey provides generous assistance to make this process easier.

## Opportunities for Summer Associates

McKinsey hires a large number of students between the first and second years of business school as summer associates. This is a great way for both the firm and the student to check each other out. If you do well, you are almost assured a full-time offer at graduation.

## Opportunities for Non-MBA Hires

In recent years, McKinsey has stepped up its efforts to bring on "diversified" (read: non-MBA) candidates for associate positions. In addition to launching glitzy on-campus recruiting programs at some of the leading law, engineering, and other graduate programs around the country, the firm has made a concerted effort to provide a clear career track for these individuals once they've joined the company. Like MBA hires, non-MBA hires typically start as associates and have the same opportunities to move up within the firm. The key difference is that non-MBAs go through a 3- to 4-week mini-MBA boot camp to learn the most important tools and concepts from business school. One alumnus of this program (with a JD) says, "You really feel like you're up to speed with the MBAs by the time you've finished." Another insider says, "We try to make sure McKinsey is friendly and open to making the transition easy for non-MBAs. We make sure that a new hire's first studies are things he can succeed at."

Insiders tell us advanced professional-degree holders (other than business, that is), now make up around 60 percent of all professionals in the firm. (The number is skewed because some countries, such as Germany, do not technically have MBA programs. Without this anomaly, the number falls to 30 or 40 percent.)

> **We try to make sure McKinsey is friendly and open to making the transition easy for non-MBAs. We make sure that a new hire's first studies are things he can succeed at.**

The Workplace

## Opportunities for Experienced Candidates

McKinsey has historically been less open to midcareer hiring than its competitors, but that's been changing in recent years. Recruiters report that experienced hires are a current focus for the firm, both experienced generalists and those with substantial industry experience. The BTO in particular is interested in candidates with graduate technical degrees and a few years of experience. Experienced hires are eligible to move up to the partner rank.

## International Opportunities

International opportunities at McKinsey are excellent. The firm recruits around the globe, and 60 percent of its revenue comes from overseas work. It has the largest international office structure of any general management consulting firm, with offices in 43 countries. There is an excellent chance that an interested employee (even a U.S. hire) could work on projects overseas or transfer to a foreign office. McKinsey has three mobility options. First, a study transfer is a single-engagement assignment paid for by the client. Such assignments generally occur when a particular office has a shortage or a consultant has special skills that justify the expense to the client. Second, a short-term transfer lasts from 9 to 18 months and is paid for by McKinsey. Consultants remain a member of their home office, but get paid out of their receiving office and get a stipend for living expenses. Short-term transfers are generally easier to obtain once an associate has become an engagement manager at the year-and-a-half level. The firm also may offer top-performing business analysts the option of a year in another country to entice them to stay on for a third year. Finally, the third option is a permanent transfer.

# Training

McKinsey invests a lot in training its employees, especially during their first year with the firm. As a new employee, you will participate in a 1-week introductory training. As you progress through the ranks at McKinsey, you'll receive 2 to 3 weeks of annual training geared toward teaching you special skills related to your particular career stage. For example, a consultant's first-year training focuses mostly on problem-solving and communication skills, while managers are trained in influencing negotiations. Recent cost cuts have meant the firm has had to cancel or combine some training programs, but training remains a high priority. McKinsey provides many practice-related training opportunities for consultants to complete of their own initiative, with ad hoc programs on such topics as PowerPoint and Excel.

An insider says, "There's an emphasis on thinking about where you are in your career and what you need to do next" during every training program. "I've been impressed with training overall" is a common insider sentiment. One insider adds, "They're great with the important stuff but kind of overlook the little things, like where's the library." If that's the worst of it, we think that's pretty good.

## Non-MBA Hires

Good news: Non-MBAs who join McKinsey are not expected to know everything about business when they walk in the door. Instead, they get pumped full of everything they need to know in a specialized "mini-MBA" training program. This intensive 3- or 4-week program helps nontraditional consultants hone their business skills with a crash course in general management and functional skills. Topics include microeconomics, finance, strategy, and specific tools such as forecasting, valuation, and discounted cashflow. One non-MBA insider says, "Your learning curve is steeper in the first year, but after that you're pretty much caught up." Those hired into the BTO will receive an additional 5-day training program on the latest technology trends and solutions. The MIT-developed program is run by MIT professors and BTO consultants.

# Insider Scoop

## What Employees Really Like

### We're Not Cheap But We're Good

McKinsey consultants talk about the excitement and importance of their engagements and the potential impact their recommendations have on client companies. As one insider says, "Companies pay us so much that they make sure we work on things that are really critical to them." Employees share a sense of pride about working for the acknowledged industry leader. More than at other firms, McKinsey projects tend to be initiated by the top management of client firms. These engagements tend to be high profile and strategic in nature, although more operational engagements are creeping into the mix.

### The Few, the Proud, the McKinseyites

Employees regularly comment on the high quality of McKinsey staff. One insider says, "Everybody here is a Rhodes scholar, a valedictorian, a class president, a member of Phi Beta Kappa, just a genius, or all of the above." Another says, "I work with people that are a lot smarter than me. A lot of people at McKinsey walk around saying, 'I was the hiring mistake.'" Constant contact with such astute colleagues offers great opportunities to learn from others and to push yourself. At the same time, one insider says, "Most McKinsey consultants I met were quite down to earth and friendly."

### Red Carpets

Insiders agree that the firm treats them very well. However, the red carpet is a little less plush than it was during the boom years—the days of all-out no-holds-barred employee-appreciation free-for-alls are gone. But the firm may allow new hires to take time off for travel before showing up for work. And McKinsey generally pulls out all the stops (or as many as are currently fiscally feasible) to make its employees happy. In addition to special treatment, McKinsey employees universally report that they're treated well day-to-day. One insider says, "There's definitely a hierarchy here, but it's not like banking, where the lowest person stays the latest and gets yelled at. People are treated as equals."

## Open Sesame

A McKinsey stint on your resume will open doors. As one insider says, "If you come to McKinsey, you can do anything with your life." McKinsey alumni have gone on to become Fortune 500 CEOs (one insider calls the firm "CEO boot camp"). "When I tell people where I work, they immediately say, 'Really?'" adds the same insider. "Nobody ever asks me what I do. Just the fact that I work at McKinsey makes them go, 'Ooh, you must be smart.'" Another insider says, "You feel like you can kick ass when you get out." McKinsey's alumni network is legendary, and the firm does all it can to help the careers of departing consultants.

## Code of Conduct

One thing that makes McKinsey stand out from the crowd is its strict code of behavior, initially set forth by father figure Marvin Bower, which continues to define how a McKinsey employee behaves. Mandatory hats for all McKinsey men went out in the '60s, but Bower's basic principles still receive the support of McKinsey staff and are communicated through stories passed down from older firm members to newbies. These principles include always putting your client's interests ahead of increasing the firm's revenues (although there has been some suggestion by outsiders that the revenues have, of necessity, taken an upper hand in some cases), never divulging information about your client, always telling the truth, never hesitating to challenge your client's opinion, and taking on engagements that are both necessary and in line with McKinsey's talents. If you like this approach, you won't find a firm that follows it more closely than does McKinsey.

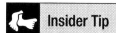
## Watch Out!

### Who's in Your Corner?

Several insiders noted that to really go places at McKinsey you need a director or principal partner in your corner. Most staffing and transfer decisions are made in unison by partner groups. "The vast majority of those partners may know you, but they may not have a strong opinion about you one way or another," says an insider. "You really need someone in the partner group to bang their fist on the table and say, 'So-and-so needs to go to Australia.' Otherwise everyone just shrugs and the decision languishes." While having a partner on your side won't guarantee your success, it will certainly improve your chances.

### Shades of the Fortune 500?

There's no doubt about it: McKinsey is the consulting firm your parents are most likely to have heard of. But with more than 7,000 employees and 650 partners, you'll never know all the other people in the organization. If you're in New York, you won't even know all the people in your office. Even if you can stand the anonymity of working in such a large organization, you may not like the corporate resistance and politics that invariably accompany size. As one insider says, "McKinsey's size and traditions make the firm less entrepreneurial than some of its elite competitors." One piece of insider advice: If the big-firm atmosphere is a downer, emphasize your interest in working at one of McKinsey's smaller offices.

### Have Suitcase, Will Travel

As at other firms, people don't always like the severe travel and work demands of consulting. "There are times when, even though you may have something planned, you just have to suck it up and stay at the office. The work has to be done, and there's nobody else but you to do it." One insider to whom we spoke has been on out-of-town engagements for nearly 2 years. And in our nomination for worst assignment imaginable, we've heard rumors about another who was assigned to an engagement on the North Slope of Alaska that lasted through most of the winter. Another insider points out, "Travel varies quite a bit region to region, but it's fairly intuitive. If you join the New York office, for instance, there's such a concentration of business there that there's no need to ever leave Manhattan. On the other hand, if you're working in New York and you're interested in the pulp and paper business, you might be on the road 4 days a week."

### The Price of Elitism

Exclusivity and elitism abound at McKinsey. What do you expect from a firm that is constantly telling its people that they are the best, that the clients it serves are the best, and that, well, everything about the firm is the best? "At times the elitist attitude rubs me the wrong way," says an insider. "It's not always the friendliest place." And don't expect McKinseyites to shift out of work mode too easily. "All conversations are about work," says an insider. "People are very driven. No one is ever talking about football or a recent movie they saw."

### If You Can't Stand the Heat . . .

Finally, several insiders commented on the negatives of consulting work in general. One insider says, "Especially as you move up into managing engagements, there is a lot of pressure." Another adds, "If you're intellectually insecure, this probably isn't the place for you. You are going to have your ideas challenged sharply and you're occasionally going to be wrong."

# Getting Hired

- The Recruiting Process

- On-the-Record Recruiter Interview

- The Interviewer's Checklist

- Interviewing Tips

- Grilling Your Interviewer

Getting Hired

# The Recruiting Process

McKinsey solicits applications from students at more than 30 U.S. MBA schools and more than 30 U.S. undergraduate programs and keeps a constant eye out for top performers. An insider says, "They'll take walk-ins from other schools, but their focus is on the Harvards, Princetons, Stanfords, and MITs of the world." And even if you are from a top school, applying for a job with McKinsey is a lot like trying to get into Harvard Medical School, Yale Law School, or Stanford Business School all over again. Many candidates packing sterling credentials will be applying from your campus—competition for the available spots is intense. But even if you're not from one of these schools, you'll still have a chance. A recruiting insider says, "Even though you might not see us on your campus, we do reach out with Web-based recruiting efforts." Of course, no matter where you come from, you're really going to have to show your recruiter what makes you special.

## Undergraduates

All applicants to McKinsey go through its formal recruiting program. At the business analyst level in the United States, the interview process involves two or three rounds of interviews, depending on which school you attend. Some interview processes begin with telephone interviews, and others begin on campus. Successful candidates in the first rounds of interviews have a final round of interviews in the office of choice. During an interview day, candidates may participate in a number of different exercises, including personal experience interviews, business case interviews, cooperative group exercises, and written cases. The interviewer is looking for excellence in problem solving, high achievement, and the ability to build strong relationships. The firm accepts applicants from any background or major.

## MBAs

The interview process for associates on U.S. campuses also takes place in two or three rounds. The first round usually involves case interviews and personal experience interviews and can take place on campus or over the telephone. Successful candidates in the first rounds of interviews at the MBA level will also have a final round of interviews in the office of choice, where they will have an opportunity to interact with office leadership and become familiar with the personality of the office.

> We look for people who value excellence and are always working to achieve it.

## Non-MBAs

As many as one-third of all new hires come from top PhD programs, engineering and science master's programs, and law and medical schools. Insiders estimate that the ratio of non-MBA associates to MBAs is close to fifty-fifty on a worldwide basis. In the United States, 30 to 40 percent of consultants are non-MBAs.

The application process for non-MBAs includes a questionnaire addressing a candidate's motivation for a career switch to consulting, as well as a few leadership and team experience questions. Non-MBA candidates can also expect a series of case interviews. However, based on our survey of McKinsey interviewees, these case questions tend to focus on issues more relevant to the candidates' academic research or personal experience than on their knowledge of business concepts. Candidates with particularly strong technology backgrounds may find opportunities in the BTO.

## Experienced Candidates

Candidates with industry experience who are interested in a spot with McKinsey should apply online at www.McKinsey.com. The online application will ask you for your geographic preference. In recent years, McKinsey has been hiring an increasing number of experienced candidates, and that trend should continue.

# On-the-Record Recruiter Interview

We designed the on-the-record recruiter interview to get you inside the recruiter's head and answer the questions you need answered to ace your interviews.

## What do you look for in a candidate's resume?

Getting a job at McKinsey isn't about crafting the perfect resume. Honors, promotions, test scores, and other academic achievements are meaningful, but they don't mean everything. We look for people who value excellence and are always working to achieve it. Please let us know what excellence means to you. Have you pursued it in school, in your work, in sports, or through service to your community? Many of our consultants have come from the top MBA programs, but we also hire many people with advanced degrees other than business degrees, including law, medicine, and doctorates. We are increasingly hiring experienced lawyers, doctors, engineers, and academics who've enjoyed successful careers in their own fields before coming to McKinsey. We welcome applicants who've achieved distinction in business and those with specialized skills and knowledge. The diverse backgrounds and varied talents of our consultants are fundamental to our success. Our differences make us a well-rounded firm and allow us to serve an increasingly exciting array of clients.

## How do you decide whether a candidate advances in the interviewing process?

Once you've applied, the appropriate recruiting team will review your application. The team will look for candidates who demonstrate skills in the following areas: problem solving, the ability to achieve goals, and influencing, leading, and building relationships with others. If your background and experience indicate a good fit, you will move forward in the interview process. This process varies depending on whether you are currently pursuing a degree (undergraduate or graduate) or are currently working.

## What's the best way to break into the interview cycle if you're not on campus?

Campus events are important, but they're not the only way to meet us. If you're no longer in school, or are enrolled at an institution where we don't currently recruit, we urge you to get in touch with us directly. Please apply online at www.McKinsey.com. The online application will ask you for your office preference. If that office is interested in pursuing your candidacy, they will be in touch to schedule the first round of interviews. In some cases, the initial interview will take place at the McKinsey office nearest to you, even if that is not the office you have selected as your preference.

## What interviewing methods does your firm use?

The interview process varies depending on whether you are a candidate currently pursuing a degree (undergraduate or graduate) or are currently working.

We often use a range of assessment techniques to try to get a holistic picture of each candidate's capabilities. In most cases, during the interview process you will have the opportunity to share important details about yourself, and you will also be given one or more business case interviews. A case is a discussion of an open-ended business situation. As you work through the business case with your interviewer, you will also become better informed about our firm and the kind of work that we do. Most candidates enjoy the cases and the business issues that they raise. Your approach to the case and the insights you reach will give you an opportunity to demonstrate your problem-solving abilities and help us get a sense of your potential. They're a way for us to see how you think on your feet, something our clients ask us to do every day. Some offices will conduct a group exercise involving more than one candidate to see how you work in that dynamic. If you're the kind of person who likes to prepare by practicing, keep the following in mind when working through some sample cases:

- Clarify the problem
- Structure the problem early and communicate your structure to the interviewer
- Ask questions but don't ask the interviewer to solve the case
- Prioritize the issues and synthesize your ideas and recommendations
- Practice

We look for balance. There is no set response, ideal background, or one right answer that gets you in the door. Most of all, we'd like to see you as you really are. Rely on your honesty, integrity, and ability to listen.

## What's the most effective way for a candidate to follow up after an interview?

McKinsey values your time and effort. It's our policy to handle each stage of the application process in a timely way, and get back to you as soon as we make our decisions; that usually means within a few days of your interview. In the event that you haven't heard from us within that time period, feel free to e-mail or call your recruiting contact.

## What is the typical career path once in the firm?

You'll benefit from extensive training and mentoring, both formal and informal, in your first few years as a consultant. As a new hire, you'll be assigned a partner who will be your advocate throughout your time at McKinsey, helping you guide your career. We'll help you sharpen your problem-solving and communication skills, and we'll provide you with feedback after each project. A more complete discussion of your progress takes place at least once a year. Together we'll explore whether you wish to experience a wide range of industries as a generalist or work toward becoming more specialized and focus on developing an area of expertise.

As a successful associate, you'll usually move into the role of engagement manager after 2 or 3 years. Over that time, you'll continue to develop as a consultant, honing your team, client, and knowledge development skills. The path to partnership varies depending on your prior work experience and on the pace of your skill development while you're here. Typically, a successful consultant can expect election to principal (partner) within 5 to 7 years after joining us. Advancing to director (senior partner) is possible after another 5 or 6 years.

## What are the qualities necessary for success in your firm?

Are you the kind of person who is willing to step outside your comfort zone to uncover new ways of doing things? Innovative solutions to complex problems are a McKinsey consultant's stock in trade. Our best candidates are passionate thinkers who care more about substance than show. They're comfortable with ambiguity and open to change.

Our consultants work in teams. We find that when you allow people with superior abilities to share their ideas, they create even better ones. You should be the kind of person who adds value not by working alone, but within a group. Your experience as both leader and participant in team dynamics—in the workplace, a class, a lab, a sport, a club—is important to us.

The qualities you bring as an individual can make or break a project. We expect that you have the integrity to refuse to cut corners. When you don't know the answer, admit it, and then do everything to find it. We offer exceptional latitude to pursue your professional passions at McKinsey, so we value people who seek, and flourish in, a trust-based environment like ours. McKinsey values original thinkers with drive, creativity, and an appetite for impact. We nourish them with challenging opportunities, a climate of meritocracy, and trust-based professional freedom.

# The Interviewer's Checklist

Interviewers use case interviews to assess a candidate's analytical abilities and conceptual skills. The interviewer also looks for leadership experience, influencing skills, and the ability to set and achieve challenging goals. Sample interview questions are available in the careers section of the McKinsey website. One interviewer warns, "Ironically, anyone who scores 'meeting qualifications' in all categories still won't go to the next round of interviews—you must be exceptional in some way to move forward."

Here's a list of additional personal factors your recruiter will be looking for in your job interview:

- Academic achievement (Have a good explanation for those B-pluses. For experienced candidates, success in the real world is more important than decade-old grades.)
- Business aptitude (It's as much how you defend it as what you say.)
- Empathy
- Leadership experience
- Ability to absorb and synthesize large amounts of information
- Personal presence
- Potential for positive impact on clients

# Interviewing Tips

1. As with any other firm, make sure you know what McKinsey does, how it's different from the competition, and why you want to work there. You can be sure that most of the people standing in line behind you do.

2. Everybody who gets a job with McKinsey has successfully answered a series of case interview questions, beginning with the very first interview. Insiders tell us that you'll do a lot better in the interview cubicle if you've worked out your case-question bugs in a practice session or three. In addition, you should make a point of attending any "crack the case" seminars sponsored by McKinsey or the other firms on your college campus, and check out McKinsey's interactive case interview on its website (www.McKinsey.com). Insiders tell us there is no single right way to answer a McKinsey case question, although there are plenty of wrong ways. However, McKinsey consultants recommend that you demonstrate your keen analytical prowess by using a framework to guide your analysis. Your framework needn't be as sophisticated as Porter's Five Forces (though if you're an MBA, you'd better at least know what the Five Forces are). Insiders also advise you to finish your answer with some workable recommendations that draw on your analysis.

3. Probably more than other firm, McKinsey looks for people who are willing to challenge conventional wisdom (and occasionally tell a CEO—politely—that you know his business better than he does). Therefore, insiders tell us that you shouldn't kowtow to your interviewer, even when the questions are aggressive. She may be testing your mental tenacity and your willingness to stand up for your opinions, as well as your grace under fire.

4. Insiders tell us that whether you're interviewing for an analyst or an associate position, one of the key qualities McKinsey seeks is leadership ability. If your resume doesn't say this loud and clear, you may not even get an interview. In any case, we recommend that you think back to situations in your personal and professional past in which you took on a leadership role. Be prepared to describe how you handled your responsibilities and discuss any challenging or difficult situations that arose.

5. Be prepared for a host of behavioral questions in your first two rounds of interviews. You may be asked questions such as, "Tell me about a time you demonstrated leadership"; "Tell me about a time you were on a team that failed"; or "I see you edited your school newspaper. What were some obstacles you faced?"

6. Charm and grooming! Think cotillion, not rave. Although dress in the U.S. offices is business casual, something more formal and conservative is a good idea for interviews.

7. Don't tell the interviewer that you're applying only to McKinsey. According to one recruiter, "Some people think it's going to be an advantage, but in reality, they aren't doing themselves any favors. It doesn't make us think you care only about us, it just calls into question your interest in consulting in general. There are a lot of solid consulting firms out there, and it's worth finding out everything you can about them." That said, you probably don't want to let on that you'd be just as happy working at Booz.

# Grilling Your Interviewer

This is your chance to turn the tables and find out what you want to know. We strongly encourage you to spend time preparing questions of your own. In the meantime, the samples below should get you started. The "Rare" questions are meant to be boring and innocuous, while the "Well Done" ones will help you put the fire to your interviewer's feet.

## Rare

- What are the advantages and disadvantages of working for McKinsey as opposed to working for a smaller, younger firm or a systems integrator?

- Where do people go after they leave McKinsey?

- What mechanisms and systems does McKinsey have to help an individual with his or her career development?

- How does McKinsey develop and maintain its intellectual capital?

- What are the hottest growth areas for the consulting industry and for McKinsey?

- Why did you decide to work for McKinsey rather than for another firm?

## Medium

- What's been done to increase the diversity of McKinsey's top ranks?

- How does McKinsey maintain a sense of community, given its size and international reach?

- What firms does McKinsey consider its primary competitors, and how does McKinsey differ from them?

- If you could have any other job, what would it be?

- How much interaction is there among the different levels within the firm?

- As the consulting industry changes, how will McKinsey continue to position itself for success?

- What's your spike?

## Well Done

- Given McKinsey's extensive database of clients as well as its tried-and-true approach, how does it keep its analysis and recommendations fresh?

- What do you do for fun?

- Do you ever feel that you have to compromise your individuality to fit in with the firm?

- How can an individual exercise his or her entrepreneurial ambitions in a firm with such a strong culture?

- What impact have economic pressures had on the culture of the firm and the kinds of engagements it is undertaking?

- What is the outlook for pure strategic consulting firms in the decade ahead?

# For Your Reference

- Recommended Reading

- For Further Study

- Key Numbers and People

# Recommended Reading

### The Will to Lead

*Martin Bower (Harvard Business School Press, 1997).*

McKinsey founder Martin Bower, in his folksy, matter-of-fact way, talks about the importance of building a network of leadership that permeates a company from top to bottom. He lays out the qualities that make an effective leader. Closely linked with these leadership characteristics are his four fundamental responsibilities of a company leader.

Bower then suggests the types of leadership teams that a well-run company might set up in making a transformation to a leadership company.

### The McKinsey Mind: Understanding and Implementing the Problem-Solving Tools and Management Techniques of the World's Top Strategic Consulting Firm

*Ethan M. Rasiel and Paul N. Friga (McGraw-Hill, 2001).*

This book follows *The McKinsey Way*, by the same authors, and offers readers a guide to understanding concepts and skills developed at McKinsey and putting them into practical action. While the first book used case studies and anecdotes from former and current McKinseyites to describe how the firm solves the thorniest business problems of their A-list clients, *The McKinsey Mind* goes a giant step further. It explains, step-by-step, how to use McKinsey tools, techniques, and strategies to solve an array of core business problems and to make any business venture more successful.

## "Why an MBA May Not Be Worth It"

While this certainly isn't what most freshly minted MBAs want to hear, the author argues that an MBA offers no guarantee of greater competence or success in the consulting industry than an undergraduate degree. She relates that during the tech bubble years, firms were forced to hire a proportionately higher number of liberal arts grads and that, with 3 weeks training, they performed at or above the level of their MBA counterparts.

Source: Anne Fisher, *Fortune*, 6/14/04.

## "The Incredible Shrinking Consultant"

This article suggests that there may be tougher times ahead for the pure-play strategy firms such as McKinsey, BCG, and Bain. As companies are watching their spending more closely, they are beginning to question the millions of dollars in fees they are spending on advice and research that is sometimes contested internally, is never implemented, or could be replicated in-house for significantly less. Warner also suggests that, faced with falling profits and shorter engagements, the consulting firms have been slow to engage in the very kind of soul searching and internal reorganization they are paid to effect in their clients.

Source: Melanie Warner, *Fortune*, 05/12/03.

## "Time for a High-Tech Shakeout"

A partner in McKinsey's San Francisco office, Mike Nevens discusses the current state of the high-tech industry. Following the burst of the bubble, he sees many companies continuing to invest in a future they are destined never to see. He explains why a shakeout is inevitable.

Source: Mike Nevens, *Financial Times*, 01/16/03.

## "The Talent Myth"

This article, which appeared in *The New Yorker*, may make anyone who has a legitimate chance at landing a job with McKinsey a little bit uneasy. It calls into question McKinsey's oft-promoted premise that hiring and encouraging "talent" (read: highly intelligent people with outstanding academic credentials) is the key underpinning to an organization's success. Enron, which became in effect a laboratory for McKinsey's talent-as-king theory, is held out as an example of what happens when coddling smart people becomes more important than focusing on organizational performance. The article raises some issues that anyone considering a career in management consulting would do well to mull over.

Source: Malcolm Gladwell, *The New Yorker*, 07/22/02.

## "The Kids in the Conference Room"

While somewhat dated, this wonderful *New Yorker* essay still rings true. The author explores the notion of McKinsey as the pinnacle of life for overachievers, those young men and women who scored straight As in grammar school, excelled at every extracurricular activity, aced the SAT, and killed in the Ivy League. The author says that to these people, "The general feeling is that in all the big wide world there are only two default fields of endeavor, as far as postgraduate employment is concerned: investment banking (ever so slightly fading) and management consulting (on the rise)." McKinsey has been ranked the favorite postgrad destination for MBAs for 4 years straight, the top firm in the top industry. McKinsey business analysts, according to the author, are all cut from the same cloth: sincere, eager, intelligent, well trained, and possessing unfocused ambition. They even talk alike. The question, in the spirit of the classic chicken-or-the-egg conundrum, is whether they were that way before they got to McKinsey or if McKinsey made them that way. The article describes an analyst's life on an engagement and neatly dismisses an analyst's job: "You are a 22-year-old business analyst after all, not a neurosurgeon." The author notes that our elite universities now function as business training grounds, rather than fertile beds of intellectualism, and that this is a departure from academia's longstanding distaste for the business world.

Source: *The New Yorker*, 10/18/99 and 10/25/99.

## "CEO Super Bowl"

Dated, but worth checking out if you want to understand why so many CEOs of top companies are former McKinseyites. *Fortune* conducts a mythical CEO Super Bowl to see which legendary name in business churns out the better CEOs: McKinsey or General Electric. For decades both GE and McKinsey have produced a remarkable number of CEOs. The comparison here is interesting because on paper McKinsey and GE could not be more different. While McKinsey prides itself on being an elitist, Ivy League-dominated firm, GE cultivates a more working-class culture that tends to be suspicious of any person holding the credentials that McKinsey covets. However, a closer look reveals that the two share a number of key similarities that may explain the remarkable success of their alumni.

Source: *Fortune*, 8/2/99.

# For Further Study

You might want to get your hands on a copy of the *McKinsey Quarterly* to learn more about the issues that McKinsey consultants have been working on lately. You can read the *Quarterly* online at www.McKinsey.com.

For insights into some of the strategic thinking at the top, read *Knowledge Unplugged: The McKinsey and Company Global Survey on Knowledge Management* by Jurgen Kluge, Wolfram Stein, and Thomas Licht (Palgrave, February 2002).

*Knowledge Unplugged* announces the results of a major survey of knowledge management practices within the most influential companies in the world. The McKinsey knowledge management team interviewed top executives and also investigated how far their plans were implemented in practice. In many companies they discovered a significant gap between the vision at the top and the reality on the shop floor. The authors argue that knowledge management is much more than simply installing a new database and can only be successful when it is at the heart of everyday personal exchanges, personal incentives, and personal responsibilities at every level of the firm.

In these uncertain times, strategic planners may want to take a gander at *20/20 Foresight: Crafting Strategy in an Uncertain World* by McKinsey partner Hugh Courtney (Harvard Press, 2001). The book grew out of McKinsey's Strategic Theory Initiative (STI). Though it may sound oxymoronic, it purports to help managers quantify uncertainty. Once a level of uncertainty is determined, managers are told to ask five central strategic planning questions: whether to shape or adapt, whether to make a move now or later, whether to focus or diversify, whether to adopt new tools and frameworks, and whether to implement new strategic-planning and decision-making processes.

Despite its unfortunate association with Enron's business model, a book called *Creative Destruction: Why Companies That Are Built to Last Underperform the Market—And How to Successfully Transform Them*, by Richard Foster and Sarah Kaplan, is a good resource for learning about how McKinsey does its work. Published in 2001, this book used McKinsey research in arguing that long-term success depends on a business's ability to transform itself, rather than change incrementally, subtly challenging the ideas in the classic *Built to Last* by Collins and Porras.

In addition to the above titles, McKinsey consultants have published a lot more books over the years. Check them out at www.McKinsey.com/knowledge/books. These titles will give you a great introduction to how McKinsey consultants write, think, and imagine the world, and provide fodder for small talk at your recruiting events.

A general resource for information about the consulting industry is put out by Kennedy Information and called Consulting Central. Its website is at www.consultingcentral.com. Kennedy Information also publishes *Consultants News*, which covers the management consulting industry.

# Key Numbers and People

While McKinsey does not make their financial information public, *Consultants News* puts together a yearly estimate based on its own research. The latest numbers were not ready as of press time, but the figures will be flat or show a slight contraction for the most recent period.

| 📁 Financial Highlights | | |
|---|---|---|
| | **2003** | **Growth (%)** |
| Revenues worldwide ($B) | 3.0 | 0 |
| Revenues U.S. ($B) | 1.0 | 0 |
| Percent of revenues from U.S. | 33 | n/a |
| Sources: WetFeet research; Consultants News. | | |

## Key People

Ian Davis, managing director

## Recruiting Contacts

McKinsey recruits at all of the big name schools (Stanford, Harvard, Wharton, Kellogg, MIT, and the like) and hires most of its consultants from the elite schools. If McKinsey comes to your campus, sign up for an on-campus interview. You can state your preference for an office location during your interview. Students at schools without campus visits should cross their fingers and apply through the firm's website, via its online application form (http://careers.McKinsey.com). A list of current job openings throughout the world can also be found at its recruiting website.

## Office Locations

McKinsey & Co. has offices in 44 countries in more than 82 cities; for a full list, see www.McKinsey.com/locations.

# WETFEET'S INSIDER GUIDE SERIES

## JOB SEARCH GUIDES

Getting Your Ideal Internship

Job Hunting A to Z: Landing the Job You Want

Killer Consulting Resumes

Killer Investment Banking Resumes

Killer Resumes & Cover Letters

Negotiating Your Salary & Perks

Networking Works!

## INTERVIEW GUIDES

Ace Your Case: Consulting Interviews

Ace Your Case II: 15 More Consulting Cases

Ace Your Case III: Practice Makes Perfect

Ace Your Case IV: The Latest & Greatest

Ace Your Case V: Return to the Case Interview

Ace Your Interview!

Beat the Street: Investment Banking Interviews

Beat the Street II: Investment Banking Interview Practice Guide

## CAREER & INDUSTRY GUIDES

Careers in Accounting

Careers in Advertising & Public Relations

Careers in Asset Management & Retail Brokerage

Careers in Biotech & Pharmaceuticals

Careers in Brand Management

Careers in Consumer Products

Careers in Entertainment & Sports

Careers in Human Resources

Careers in Information Technology

Careers in Investment Banking

Careers in Management Consulting

Careers in Manufacturing

Careers in Marketing & Market Research

Careers in Nonprofits & Government

Careers in Real Estate

Careers in Supply Chain Management

Careers in Venture Capital

Consulting for PhDs, Doctors & Lawyers

Industries & Careers for MBAs

Industries & Careers for Undergrads

## COMPANY GUIDES

Accenture

Bain & Company

Boston Consulting Group

Booz Allen Hamilton

Citigroup's Corporate & Investment Bank

Credit Suisse First Boston

Deloitte Consulting

Goldman Sachs Group

J.P. Morgan Chase & Company

Lehman Brothers

McKinsey & Company

Merrill Lynch

Morgan Stanley

25 Top Consulting Firms

Top 20 Biotechnology & Pharmaceuticals Firms

Top 25 Financial Services Firm